MEXICO CITY

TRAVEL GUIDE 2023

90+ Ultimate Mexico City Experiences (With Pictures), Your Guide to All You Need to Know, where to Go, what to Do and Local Tips.

ADVENTURE PLANET

TABLE OF CONTENTS

MEXICO CITY IMAGES

A TRAVELLER'S EXPERIENCE

The sun was shining brightly as I stepped off the plane and onto the tarmac in Mexico City. I was here to experience a culture and a way of life that I had only ever dreamed of. I had been curious about Mexico City for a long time and was excited to finally get the chance to explore it.

I had read up on the city and did my best to prepare for the experience. I had heard the stories of the vibrant culture, the delicious food, the beautiful architecture and the friendly people. Now I was here to experience these things for myself.

As I made my way through the bustling streets of the city, I was taken aback by the vibrancy and energy of the place. Everywhere I looked there was something new and exciting. I felt like I was walking through a living painting. Everywhere I looked I could see evidence of a rich and vibrant culture. I was mesmerized by the colorful murals, the cheerful people, and the delicious smell of street food.

I soon discovered that Mexico City was a great place to explore. I spent my days wandering through the city and discovering the hidden gems it had to offer. From the ancient ruins of Teotihuacan to the bustling markets of Coyoacan, I found something to keep me enthralled every day.

It wasn't just the sights that I enjoyed, but also the people. Everywhere I went I was greeted with a warm and friendly smile. I was fascinated by the way the locals interacted with one another, and the way they were so passionate about their lives. I found myself wanting to learn more about the culture, the language, and the way of life.

The time I spent in Mexico City was a truly incredible experience. I made so many memories and learned so much about the place and its culture. I was able to experience a culture and a way of life that I had only ever dreamed of, and I found myself longing to go back and explore more. Mexico City is truly a magical place, and I am so thankful for the time I spent there.

-Laura..

ABOUT MEXICO CITY

Mexico City is an intense and eclectic city, boasting a population of over 20 million. It is a major economic and cultural hub in Latin America, comprised of colonial-style architecture, luxurious residential areas, and other parts of the city where urbanization has taken its toll.

The city has a long and complicated history, having been founded by the Aztecs before they were conquered by Spanish conquistadores in the 16th century. Recent excavations have uncovered some of the remains of the Great Pyramid of Tenochtitlán, and new constructions in the city often reveal further pieces of the ancient city.

Modern day Mexico City is a vibrant place, with affluent and poorer areas existing side by side. Hip and stylish districts such as La Condesa and Colonia boast lively cafes and bars, beautiful colonial architecture and a thriving nightlife. The south of the city is home to several wealthy enclaves, as well as the University City and the former home of Frida Kahlo. The north and east have more challenging areas, but there are plenty of sites of cultural importance to be discovered across the city.

Mexican cuisine is renowned around the globe, and Mexico City is the perfect place to experience it. From street stalls to hole-in-the-wall eateries to upscale restaurants, you can find all kinds of delicious food here. There are also plenty of international offerings available, especially Western European and Japanese cuisine, which are popular among the city's growing middle class.

Mexico City is also home to some of the world's largest city parks, such as the Bosque de Chapultepec and Desierto de los Leones. You can also take a ride on a trajinera (barge) to explore Xochimilco, the ancient canal system that used to surround the original Aztec city. Although the Spaniards drained the lake that provided protection for the city shortly after the conquest, you can still get a glimpse into the city's past. However, due to the growing population, the water levels are being reduced as aquifers are being drained, which is causing the city to sink.

HISTORY OF MEXICO CITY

Mexico City has a remarkable history that began with the founding of the Aztec city of Tenochtitlán in the middle of Lake Texcoco. Its architecture and engineering were so awe-inspiring that some of the first Spanish men to witness it were left wondering if they were dreaming. Despite its location in the lake, Cortés and his followers managed to conquer the city in 1525, largely due to an ancient prophecy that Moctezuma, the Aztec king, believed to be coming true. He thought of Cortés as the feathered serpent-god, Quetzalcóatl, who was prophesied to reclaim his throne in 1519, the year that Cortés arrived in Mexico. After being courted by the Aztec ruler, the Spanish were able to easily overthrow the empire. Although most of Tenochtitlán has been destroyed, excavations have revealed some of the glories of the city that still remain beneath the surface.

As Mexico City began to emerge, it soon had the biggest population of people of mixed European and indigenous descent in New Spain. A social hierarchy developed, with those born in Spain at the top, and the criolles (those of up to 1/8 indigenous heritage) in second place. After Mexico achieved independence in 1821, it was followed by a few decades of war with the United States, which ended with Mexico City being briefly occupied and California, New Mexico and Texas being given away. This was followed by internal struggles, culminating in the revolution of 1910, which resulted in the country being ruled by the PRI (Institutional Revolutionary Party) for 71 years. It wasn't until 2000 that another party came to power, though in 2012 the PRI returned. Nowadays, Mexico City, one of the biggest cities globally, is home to the whole federal government.

Are You Aware That:

- The history of Mexico City (or Tenochtitlán) is based on an old prophecy? It is said that the Mexica saw an eagle consuming a snake while perched on a cactus on an island in Lake Texcoco, which is now represented on the Mexican flag.

• The Paseo road in Kansas City was modeled after the famous Paseo de la Reforma in Mexico City.

• The Spanish drained a large portion of the lake that surrounded the city, although it is now said to be sinking. It is believed that it has gone down by almost 10 meters in the 20th century.

MEXICO CITY WEATHER

In Mexico City, the period from **April to June** is the warmest and most arid of the year, but the altitude keeps temperatures at a pleasant 26°C (79°F). Despite this, showers in the afternoon or evening are relatively common in the months from **June to October**.

Visiting the city during the week before Easter (Semana Santa) is recommended if you want to experience Mexico City at its best. From **November to February**, the temperature is cooler at around 20°C (69°F), although this is usually the time of year when air pollution is at its highest.

VISA AND PASSPORT REQUIREMENTS FOR MEXICO

	Passport Required	Return Ticket Required	Visa Required
USA	Yes	Yes	No
British	Yes	Yes	No
Canadian	Yes	Yes	No
Australian	Yes	Yes	No
EU	Yes	Yes	No

Passports

A passport valid for the length of your stay is needed for citizens listed in the chart.

Visas

Visas are not required for citizens listed in the chart above for touristic or business purposes. When arriving in Mexico, the

Migration official will decide the amount of time permitted to stay in the country.

Visitors, both tourists and business travelers, have a maximum stay of six months. You should acquire a landing card valid for 180 days online, from your airline on direct flights, or when entering by land at an INM office. It may be necessary to show a return/onward ticket and evidence of financial means. You must hold onto your landing card throughout your stay since you will need to present it when you depart.

Cruise ship passengers of all nationalities are exempt from a visa when staying within the boundaries that the Mexican government and the cruise ship company have agreed upon.

Visa Note

People who are not listed in the chart should get in touch with the embassy to find out the visa necessities for Mexico.

Cost and Validity

Tourist visas cost £43.77 and are valid for a period of up to six months.

Application to

Applications should be made to the consulate or the consular part of the embassy.

Working days

It usually takes two working days for the visa to be processed.

Sufficient Funds

Visitors who need a visa must show their pay slips and bank statements from the last six months prior to submitting their application.

Entry with children

For those traveling with children, Mexican authorities have revoked the requirement to have a notarised permission slip from their parents for them to leave the country; this is only applicable to Mexican citizens or those residing in Mexico on a permanent or temporary basis.

Entry with pets

For those bringing pets into the country, they must present a veterinary certificate to the Office of Agriculture and Health Inspection at the port of entry. This must show that the animal has been inspected, is in good health and has been vaccinated against rabies.

MEXICO'S MONEY AND DUTY-FREE

Currency information

Mexico has its own currency, the Mexican Peso (abbreviated as MXN and denoted by M$). Each Peso is divided into 100 centavos. You can find Peso notes of M$1,000, 500, 200, 100, 50 and 20. Coins are available in the following values: M$10, 5, 2, 1, in addition to 50 and 20 centavos.

Be aware that the M$1,000 and M$500 notes may be difficult to exchange in some places, and not accepted at all in others.

Credit cards

Credit cards such as Mastercard, Visa and American Express are typically accepted by businesses catering to travelers, like car rental agencies, airlines, some bus lines, and higher-end hotels, shops, and restaurants. Though credit companies may add a surcharge of around 5% for foreign transactions. For humbler establishments, it is necessary to have pesos to make a purchase.

ATM

In many cities and villages in Mexico, there are ATMs on the Cirrus and Plus networks that give out pesos to cardholders of debit and credit cards.

Travellers cheques

Since the prevalence of ATMs and credit cards, traveler's cheques have become less necessary to carry money, though they can be cashed in exchange houses and are accepted as readily as US Dollar traveler's cheques, in Pounds Sterling and Euros.

Banking hours

Banks are typically open from 9:00am to 4:00pm Monday through Friday, while some are open longer hours and others open on Saturday mornings.

Currency restrictions

No restrictions are placed on bringing in or taking out local or foreign currency, though any amount equivalent to US$10,000 or more must be declared. The amount that can be taken out of the country must be no more than the amount declared upon import.

Currency exchange

The US dollar is very popular in Mexico, so much so that it can be hard to pay in pesos. Exchange houses offer a better rate of exchange than hotels, and they also provide a faster service than banks. Not all banks in Mexico can exchange money.

Mexico Duty-Free

Travellers over 18 years of age are allowed to bring into Mexico up to:

- 25 cigas, 10 packs of cigarettes or 200g of tobacco
- 3L of spirits and 6L of wine
- Other goods with a value of up to US$500 (if arriving by air) or US$300 (if arriving by land). During holiday periods such as Easter week, Mexican nationals are allowed to bring up to US$500 worth of goods when arriving by land.

Banned Imports

Certain items are prohibited from being imported into the country, including images depicting childhood in a degrading manner, narcotics, live species of predatory fish, used clothing not considered to be part of a person's personal luggage, firearms and ammunition.

Banned Exports

Archaeological artefacts

DO'S AND DON'TS FOR VISITING MEXICO CITY

Before you embark on your journey to Mexico City, it is important to be informed about the local area. Mexico City is a big and vibrant financial and cultural center, so it's wise to brush up on some Dos and Don'ts to ensure your trip goes smoothly.

Be aware of the currency (the Mexican peso) and the official language (Spanish), as well as the many indigenous languages that are still spoken in the city. Additionally, it is important to find a place to stay and get acquainted with the city before you visit. Finally, be sure to avoid rookie mistakes (like gulping tap water after a spicy meal) to ensure you have an enjoyable trip. This list will aid you in recognizing any areas of not knowing so that you can take full advantage of your vacation.

- **Residents of Mexico City Are Commonly Referred to as Chilangos.**

Residents of Mexico City are generally known as chilangos. The US is similarly called gringolandia. Though the terms can be used positively or in a derogatory way, it's best to take them with a grain of salt.

- **Avoid The Subway During Rush Hour.**

To avoid feeling overwhelmed and frustrated on the metro, it's recommended to avoid travelling during rush hour (6am to 9am and 6pm to 9pm). If you can, plan your trips around these peak times to ensure a smoother journey.

- **Sample Their Amazing Cuisine**

If you're planning a trip to Mexico, make sure you take the opportunity to sample their amazing cuisine. From street food like tortas, tacos and tamales, to the more traditional dishes found in Mexican restaurants, there's something to suit everyone's tastes. When selecting a food vendor, it's best to pick the ones that look busy and popular. You can be certain that you are receiving the greatest quality in this approach.

- **Tortillas, Corn, And Chili Are Essential Ingredients in Their Culinary.**

The base of most Mexican food is made up of three key ingredients - tortillas, corn and chilli. If you're not a fan of these flavours, it's time to get used to them, as they form the basis of most dishes. Tacos, gorditas and tlayudas are just some of the delicious meals you can expect to find. However, when ordering quesadillas in Mexico City, remember to ask for them with cheese, as it's not added automatically. Also, be aware that they tend to add chilli to everything - even fruit!

- **Be Discerning When Trying Spicy Foods**

When it comes to Mexican cuisine, it is important to be discerning when trying spicy foods. It's good practice to ask for any spicy ingredients on the side, allowing you to add them in moderation without ruining the meal. If you're a fan of spice, feel free to test the waters but be aware that the spicy standards may be different than what you're used to.

- **Do Not Drink Tap Water**

Additionally, do not drink tap water, as it could make you sick, and be mindful of other ways you might ingest it. This includes what your salad is washed in, as well as refraining from accepting ice cubes. Even if you take all the necessary precautions, you may still experience an upset stomach during your stay, so it's best to avoid eating street food and drink plenty of rehydrating electrolytes.

- **The National Beer of the Country Is Not Corona**

Despite Corona being a widely available and popular beer outside of Mexico, it is not the national beer of the country. In fact, the national drink of Mexico is tequila! That being said, there are still plenty of Cervezas to choose from, such as Modelo, Tecate, Victoria and Sol.

- **Tip A Minimum of 10 Percent in Bars and Restaurants**

When it comes to tipping in restaurants and bars, it is not as important as it is in the United States. Generally, it is appropriate to tip a minimum of 10 percent for servers and those who bring the bill. Usually, tipping is not expected at street-food stalls and for taxi drivers, although your tips will still be welcome.

- **Do Not Take Taxis from The Roadside**

It's essential to be aware of your surroundings when travelling to a new city, especially when it comes to taking taxis. To avoid the risks associated with kidnapping, it is best to only use official cab stands, such as at airports, or use services like Uber.

- **Research The Different Neighborhoods**

Before visiting a new city, it's important to research the different neighborhoods and their safety levels. Mexico City is commonly known for its relatively safe areas such as Roma, Condesa, Coyoacán and Polanco, but if you do decide to venture further afield, it is important to check the most recent news and trends on reliable websites.

- **The Historic Center of the City Is Only One Aspect of the City; There's Much More to Explore.**

Visitors to Mexico City tend to head straight to the popular tourist attractions when they arrive, such as the monuments, destinations, and well-known restaurants in the city's historic center. But there's much more to explore in this large metropolis than the Zócalo and the downtown area. Venture south to see San Ángel or Xochimilco canals, or head north to Santa María la Ribera.

- **Mexico City Is Not the Same as Cancún**

It's important to remember that Mexico City is not the same as Cancún - the capital can get quite chilly, with plenty of rain from June to September. So, it's wise to check the local weather forecast before packing your bags. Also, shorts are not typically worn by people in this area.

- **Don't Flush Your Used Toilet Paper**

Make sure you don't flush your used toilet paper in Mexico City as the plumbing systems here are not designed to cope with it. Instead, bin the tissue in the cubicle.

- **The City Is Prone to Earthquakes**

Be aware that the city is prone to earthquakes and the residents are well trained in what to do if one is predicted. The alarm will sound approximately 20 seconds before it is expected to hit and you should head to the nearest meeting point. Be prepared and stay safe!

- **Mexican Spanish Is Distinct from Castellano**

If you are a Spanish speaker who has been exposed to peninsular Spanish, then getting to Mexico could be a bit of a shock. Not only does the accent differ, with more 's' sounds than its peninsular counterpart, but the vocabulary also varies. Some words you need to be aware of are; mande ('pardon?'), ahorita (literally 'right now,' but in practice anywhere from 'now' to 'never'), camion ('bus') and con permiso ('excuse me,' as in 'can I get past you?').

And don't try to use the word coger, as it means something inappropriate in Mexico.

- **When It Comes to Swear Words, Chingar Is the One You Should Know.**

This term is widely used in Mexico, heard between friends, shouted from car windows and at football games. It is used to express anger and frustration, with expressions like chingue a su madre (go fuck yourself) and vete a la chingada (also, go fuck yourself). Other popular swear words are pendejo and hijo de su puta madre.

- **September 16 Is The Date Celebrated as Independence Day, Not May 5.**

This doesn't need any explanation

- **Abstain from Consuming Tequila in A Single Gulp**

Rather than drinking tequila quickly, it is customary to savor it slowly and sip it.

YOUR PACKING CHECKLIST FOR THE CLIMATE AND CULTURE OF MEXICO CITY

I f you're heading to Mexico City, it's important to plan accordingly and bring along the right clothing to ensure you can explore comfortably. Contrary to common belief, Mexico City is not as hot as other Mexican areas like Baja or Tulum since it is situated at an elevation of 7,350ft (2,250m). Therefore, when deciding what to pack for your trip, you should take into consideration the climate, safety, culture, and comfort. It may seem like a lot of factors to consider, but this chapter will break down everything you need to know about how to dress for the weather, culture, and safety no matter the time of year.

The Climate in Mexico City

The climate in Mexico City can vary depending on the time of year you visit.

- **Summer/Rainy Months, From May to October**

During the summer months, from May to October, the weather is typically hot and humid. This is the rainy season, with a heavy rain shower potentially occurring after 5pm each day. The temperature usually varies between 79°F (26°C) and 55°F (12°C) during this time.

- **Winter/ Dry Season in Mexico City (October-May)**

The dry season in Mexico City (October-May) is typically a great time to visit if you'd rather avoid unexpected rain showers. The days are warm, with temperatures around 73°F (23°C) and nights are cool, with temperatures around 41°F (5°C). In December, visitors are often surprised by the chill in the air, but this is also when the sky is its bluest and the city is most beautiful. It's important to dress accordingly; layers are a must.

Regardless of when you choose to visit, you can expect pleasant weather with minimal variance year-round. Temperatures are generally mild and consistent, making Mexico City an enjoyable city to explore any time of year.

What to Wear in Mexico City During the Summer (Wet Season)

When it comes to what to wear in Mexico City during the summer (wet season), jeans are the go-to choice for many locals. They are comfortable and offer enough warmth for the cooler nights. But if you prefer, shorts, dresses, and skirts are also great options. The main idea is to dress in layers. This way, you can add and remove pieces of clothing depending on how hot or cold it gets during the day. An umbrella or raincoat is also a must-have in the summer since it rains so often. And lastly, a light jacket is a great choice to bring along in case it gets a bit chilly in the shade or during the night.

What to Wear in Mexico City During the Winter (Dry Season)

Mexico City's winters, while mild compared to other places, can still be quite chilly, especially in the mornings and evenings. To ensure that you stay comfortable when out and about, layers are key - make sure to bring a jacket and light sweaters to wear as temperatures can range from the mid-40s Fahrenheit (single digits in Celsius) to the high 60s or 70s Fahrenheit. The dry season typically runs from December to January - the coldest months - so if you're visiting during this time, pack accordingly.

I personally stick to jeans, a warm jacket, and either a short-sleeve top or sweater for the day. That way, I'm able to adjust my outfit to the changing temperatures, allowing me to enjoy the city without being too cold or too warm.

Do I Have to Dress in A Conservative Manner?

No, you don't have to dress in a conservative manner when you're in Mexico City. In fact, it's a very multicultural city with people that embrace unique hairstyles, piercings, tattoos, and more.

Shorts, dresses, skirts, or sleeveless tops could make you stand out, but it also depends on the location you're in. To be on the safe side, you may want to opt for something a bit more covered up if you plan to use public transport or be in more crowded areas like the Historic Center. Although it's uncommon, there have been cases of verbal and physical harassment in the city, so it's best to be aware of your surroundings. In conclusion, you do not need to dress conservatively in Mexico City, but it's good to be mindful of where you are and what you're wearing.

What to Wear at a Mexican Bar?

If you're looking to explore Mexico City's vibrant nightlife, you'll find plenty of great bars and clubs to check out. Generally speaking, the dress code is fairly casual, though this can vary depending on where you're going. Neutrals are the way to go when it comes to colors, and you don't need to worry about going overboard with jewelry. Polanco is the more upscale area, while Roma and Condesa have a more urban and trendy vibe. Don't forget to bring a light jacket though, as the streets can get quite chilly during the night.

What to Bring to Mexico City

- **Jeans**

Jeans are an absolute must-have for those visiting Mexico City; they are incredibly comfortable, stylish enough to fit in with the locals, and great for cycling or using public transport. You should definitely include them in your packing list.

- **T-Shirts and Tanks**

T-shirts and tanks are also suitable for the city's mild climate - in the hotter months, you may even want to opt for something strapless or with thinner straps. In Mexico City, women are more likely to display their shoulders or tummies than their legs.

- **Dresses and Skirts**

In Mexico City, I tend to stay away from wearing dresses and skirts for comfort reasons. They can be great for dressing up or looking nice for pictures, but it's not something I would consider essential. If you don't like jeans, however, then a dress or skirt is totally fine. It's important to make sure they are at least knee or ankle-length though, as the beach is the only place where shorter hemlines are acceptable.

- **Jacket**

No matter the season, I would highly recommend bringing a jacket. On my first trip here I made the mistake of thinking I could get away with shorts and a t-shirt in November - I was wrong! Bring a light pullover for summer and a warm coat for winter. You probably won't need it during the day, but it's important to have for the colder mornings and evenings.

- **Comfortable Shoes**

Bringing a pair of shoes designed for comfort while walking is essential for a trip to Mexico City. I usually opt for sneakers or boots, as they're the most supportive and hygienic options. Open-toe shoes are usually less supportive, and can leave you more exposed to any dirt in the city. During the summer months and the rainy season, sandals can be impractical, leaving your feet exposed to potentially dirty city water.

- **Sunglasses and/or A Hat**

The sun is very strong in Mexico City, so it's a good idea to bring sunglasses or a hat to protect yourself from squinting in the Historic Center and other areas with fewer trees and taller buildings.

- **Raincoat or Umbrella**

If you're planning a trip to Mexico during the summer, you'll need to bring along a raincoat or umbrella. Generally, you'll be fine in the morning and afternoon without one, however, it's wise to have one on hand after 4 or 5 pm. Although the rainstorms don't usually last for very long, when it rains in Mexico City, it's usually a downpour.

- **Jewelry**

When it comes to jewelry, my advice is to keep it simple. Wearing flashy gold or diamond jewelry is not a good idea. I once saw a man have his gold chain ripped off his neck, even in a relatively safe area. A safer option would be to wear simple gold earrings, a thin necklace or even a gold wedding band. These items won't attract too much attention.

Packing Electronics Travel Accessories

- **Portable Power Bank:** A portable power bank is ideal for when you're on the go, be it a flight or a day trip, so that your gadgets can maintain their charge.

- **Spare Plug and Charger Cable:** it's wise to bring a spare plug and a lengthy charger cable in case there's no outlet nearby your bed.

- **Electronic Door Alarm:** if you're traveling alone, it might be beneficial to bring an electronic door alarm to help you get a better night's sleep.

- **Kindle:** If you're looking for a way to enjoy your spare time, why not pick up a Kindle? The latest Paperwhites are both waterproof and perfect for reading in bright sunlight.

- **Hotspot:** When travelling to Mexico, you may find it difficult to access the internet in certain areas, such as Tulum. If you need to work remotely from there, then it may be worth investing in a hotspot.

- **Smartphone:** To make the most of your trip, make sure to check out any apps I recommend specifically for Mexico travel, as they can help you plan and manage your journey.

- **Camera:** Although modern phones are able to take great pictures, if you're looking to capture underwater videos or action shots, then you should consider bringing along a GoPro or other video camera.

What Else to Pack

Don't forget the normal travel necessities, such as:

- Passport and a separate copy of your passport
- Toiletries (Shampoo, conditioner, toothbrush, toothpaste, soap, and razor)
- Underwear
- Socks (if you're bringing sneakers)
- Headphones
- Water Bottle
- Sunscreen and bug spray
- Daypack and travel backpack

Apps for Traveling to Mexico

Getting suitable applications on your mobile phone is almost as essential as packing the appropriate items in your bag. A few apps that are beneficial for travelling to Mexico include:

- **Uber (IOS | Android):** It is both secure and available in Mexico City.

- **Restorando (Android):** This is a great choice for making reservations at restaurants, although please note that The Fork has acquired Restorando, so it no longer operates independently.

- **Duolingo (IOS | Android):** Allows those still learning Spanish to do so in an entertaining manner, mastering new vocabulary and grammar.

- **Google Translate (Available On Both IOS and Android):** This will come in handy. Download the Spanish language pack prior to your visit so you can translate signs, menus, and conversations even when you don't have access to WiFi or data.

I hope you find this useful and that it has piqued your interest in visiting Mexico City. With the weather being beautiful throughout the year, it's important to remember to bring an umbrella for summer and a warm coat for winter. Layering is key regardless of the season, and you can dress however you prefer, whether it be casual or fancy. Exploring Mexico City is an amazing experience, and it can be even more enjoyable if you're prepared and dressed appropriately.

NAVIGATING MEXICO CITY: A COMPREHENSIVE GUIDE TO PUBLIC TRANSPORTATION

Mexico City is an incredible city with nine million inhabitants in the city centre, and over 22 million in the wider metropolitan area. As such, it can be very intimidating for first-time visitors to figure out how to get around. But, you'll be pleased to know that there are plenty of excellent transport options available for tourists who wish to explore the city and its many wonderful neighborhoods.

In this chapter, we'll provide a comprehensive look at the best methods of transport in Mexico City. All of these can be used to get around the city and visit the major attractions. For those looking to venture further out into the suburbs, there are other transport types available, but these can be a bit complicated and unnecessary for visitors.

So, if you're wondering what the best way to get around Mexico City is, read on.

METRO

For those on a budget, Mexico City's Metro is the most affordable way to get around the city. The system is made up of 12 colour-coded lines, with most of them running underground. This avoids the heavy traffic that can be found in some parts of the city. A single ticket to ride the Metro **costs only 5 pesos** and can be purchased with cash at the ticket desks at the station. Alternatively, visitors staying in the city longer than a few days can invest in **a smart card (tarjeta) which costs 10 pesos** and can be used to pay for all forms of public transport. The card can be shared between multiple people as long as each person taps the card when they enter the station. **On weekdays, the Metro opens at 5 a.m.; on weekends, it opens at 6 a.m.; and on holidays, it opens at 7 a.m.** Services stop at midnight every night. Transfers inside the station are free.

Once you use a ticket to enter the station, it's cost-free to switch to other lines as many times as desired. You won't be charged again so long as you remain inside the station.

The directional signs and maps in the platforms and trains make it very simple to navigate. We also found Google Maps very useful in planning our journey. Just type in the starting point and destination and it will give the exact instructions for which line to take and the transfers you need to make.

The trains come every few minutes, though there can be delays or a buildup of passengers during rush hour. Normally, you shouldn't have to wait longer than five minutes for a train. Mexico City has efficient public transportation!

It can get really crowded during rush hour, and most blogs advise to avoid it. This usually occurs between 7 am - 9 am and 5 pm - 7 pm. But the great thing about the system is that if one train is too full, you can always wait a few minutes until the next one arrives.

Regardless of the time of day you are travelling on the Metro, be mindful of your belongings just as you would in any crowded environment in any city. Hold your bag in front of you and keep any phones or wallets in a secure place. Although caution should always be taken, I have never felt uneasy while riding on the Metro, which is still the most convenient and economical way to navigate Mexico City.

Additionally, some trains feature a special carriage designated for women and children, identifiable by a pink colour. Platforms usually have markers that indicate where these carriages will arrive, so it is easy to locate them. If you are a solo female traveller or a group of female companions, I highly recommended taking advantage of these carriages for extra peace of mind.

TREN LIGERA (LIGHT RAIL)

The Tren Ligera, otherwise known as the Xochimilco Light Rail, is an offshoot of the Mexico City Metro. There is one line which runs from Tasqueña Metro Station to Xochimilco, home of the Canals of Xochimilco. This route also passes by Estadio Azteca, the country's largest stadium and the home ground for two of the city's famous soccer teams, Club America and Cruz Azul.

Riding the Tren Ligera will cost you just 3 pesos, but unlike the Metro, you must use a smart card to make the payment. Paper tickets are not available, so you will need to purchase **a 10 pesos smart card** if you want to use the light rail. The Tren Ligera **operates during the same hours as the Metro.**

METROBUS

Mexico City's Metrobus system is a relatively new form of public transportation. It consists of seven color-coded lines that span across the city, and unlike regular buses, they have a dedicated lane on the road, so they can avoid traffic congestion. The buses are usually long and bendy in the middle, and Line 7 even uses double-decker buses.

Metrobus stops are more like 'stations', with raised platforms and ticket machines. The **fare is 6 pesos per trip** and a smart card is required; no paper tickets are accepted. Popular roads like Paseo de la Reforma and Avenida Insurgentes both have Metrobus lines running along them.

If you are based in Roma Norte or Condesa, the Metrobus is the most efficient way to travel around Mexico City. As the Metro stations in these neighbourhoods aren't ideally placed, the Metrobus goes along Avenida Insurgentes, which cuts right through the centre. Every journey is 6 pesos, and you can transfer to other Metrobus lines within two hours of touching on without additional cost. To make your travels easier whilst in Mexico City, buy a smart card on your first day; it can be topped up, shared with a travelling companion and is used to access all types of transport.

The Metrobus runs from 4:30am Monday – Saturday, and from 5am on Sundays and holidays, until midnight. Though certain stations have different opening hours in the morning, it shouldn't be a problem for tourists. There is a designated area for women and children, just like on the Metro, though it can get very crowded during peak times. Personally, I would rather be on the Metro than the Metrobus during peak hours, but both offer great efficiency and low fares regardless of the time of day.

ECOBICI BICYCLE

EcoBici is Mexico City's amazing bike-share system and is undoubtedly the best way to explore the city! Everything is incredibly well organised, with over 600 EcoBici stations and 9,000 bikes available. You can easily sign up for an account online - the website is straightforward and even shows up in English. You can choose between one, three or seven-day passes, or even an annual pass, which offers great value if you're in the city for more than a week. At the time of writing, prices are;

- 118 pesos for one day ($6)
- 234 pesos for three days ($12)

- 391 pesos for seven days ($20)
- 521 pesos for an annual pass ($26).

The bikes are **available from 5 am until 12:30 am,** so you can really make the most of your time in Mexico City!

Once you have your account set up, get the app and log in. You will be able to view a map of all the bike stations in the city (over 600!), as well as an up-to-date count of how many bikes are in each station. With more than 9,000 bikes around the city, you can usually find one close by.

When you select a bike at a station, open the app, scan the QR code and the bike will be discharged. You have two minutes to make sure the bike fits your needs (quickly jump on and adjust the seat, if needed), and if not, you can return it and take another one.

Once you are ready to go, you have 45 minutes to ride the bike to your destination without any extra charges. This is to ensure that the bikes are being used for short-distance trips, and not kept out for an extended period of time.

If you need to go further than 45 minutes, you can easily find a station, return your bike and grab a new one. With stations scattered all around, you can ride past many of them on your way. You can take as many rides as you would like (within the 45-minute time limit) with your chosen rental pass.

When you get to your final stop, simply dock the bike in an open space at a station and you'll hear a notification noise indicating that it has been returned properly. Mexico City's bike-sharing program runs from 5am to 12:30am, allowing you to explore at any time of the day or night. On Sunday mornings, Paseo de la Reforma, one of the busiest roads in Mexico, is closed to cars, permitting locals to go out and take a stroll, go for a jog, or rent an EcoBici and cycle down the tree-lined street surrounded by tall buildings.

Biking in Mexico City can be intimidating initially, but after getting used to it, you'll find it to be quite enjoyable. The majority of main roads, such as Paseo de la Reforma, have bike lanes or wide sidewalks, making it secure and uncomplicated to navigate. Although the bike isn't ideal for every part of the city, it is still a great way to move between different neighbourhoods. Cut down travelling time between areas and when you arrive, park the bike and explore on foot.

TAXI

Taxis in Mexico City can be a bit of a risky business. Many of them are unregistered and tourists are often charged an exorbitant amount for the ride. It is recommended to avoid taking a taxi if you can and instead opt for Uber or DiDi. If you have to take one, it is best to order it through a reputable business like a hotel or shopping centre, or through a sitio, which is a taxi stand where you pay in advance and your trip is recorded. Do not just pick up a taxi from the street.

When you do get into the taxi, be sure to agree on the price before the journey starts. If the driver is reluctant to do so, it is probably best to just walk away. The meters are rarely used, and if they insist on using the meter, it is likely to be tampered with. Overall, taxis in Mexico City can be more expensive and dangerous than rideshare services, so it is best to be aware of the risks before hopping in one.

From our experience, it is best to stay away from taking a taxi. Utilizing Uber or DiDi gives you the convenience of entering your destination in the language you are familiar with, and using the map to keep track of where you are headed. If you do not speak Spanish, information can be easily misconstrued, and it can be difficult to explain to a taxi driver where you want to go.

However, if you find yourself in a situation where you need to take a taxi, make sure to adhere to the following advice for a safe and reasonably priced journey.

RIDESHARE

Rideshare services like Uber and DiDi make getting around Mexico City an easy and convenient option. These services are popular around the world, and in Mexico City, they provide a great alternative to walking or taking public transport. You just need to order the vehicle via the app, or pay cash directly to the driver.

However, it's important to bear in mind that rideshare drivers are on the roads, and subject to the same traffic conditions as regular cars. This means that your journey may take longer than anticipated, especially in a city like Mexico City where the traffic is notoriously bad.

Uber is still the most common rideshare option in Mexico City, but DiDi is quickly becoming a strong competitor. There are thousands of drivers available, and it is usually fast and affordable to order a ride. Paying for the ride is straightforward too; you can pay via the app, or with cash directly to the driver.

In Mexico City, Uber and DiDi are generally cheaper than taking a taxi, although prices can go up at peak times. We advise that you download both apps to compare the prices and waiting times, particularly during busy periods. Unlike many other countries, you can pay for Uber rides in cash in Mexico City, although you should always make sure you have the correct change or be ready to not receive any change. If you have an Uber account with a connected PayPal or credit card, it is much more straightforward to use this payment method rather than use cash.

I typically use Uber in the evenings, as the Metro still runs, and there are still a lot of people out and about late in the night. But I feel safer taking an Uber from Point A to Point B at night, and it also saves time walking to and from the Metro station.

DRIVING

Despite Mexico City's large size and chaotic hustle and bustle, driving is not a method of transport we would advocate. The traffic is usually congested and navigating can be a challenge, even with GPS or a partner acting as navigator. Parking is difficult to find and can be expensive, as some areas require payment by the hour.

Furthermore, the cost of renting a car and petrol is significantly more expensive than using public transport or ride-sharing services. Thus, unless you have a cool head and top notch driving skills, it's probably not worth the hassle.

WALKING

When it comes to exploring Mexico City's neighbourhoods, walking is the best way to go. Most roads have safe, wide sidewalks, making it a great option as it's free and a great form of exercise. You can take your time and gain a better insight into the city that you wouldn't be able to experience from underground or from a vehicle.

The sidewalks are wide and many major avenues have pedestrian sections in the middle and outer edges of the road. Not to mention the parks, which can be great shortcuts and sightseeing spots. Depending on the area, it is generally safe to walk around during the evening until around 10 pm, as there are usually still plenty of people coming home from work or dining out. After this time, you might want to opt for an Uber or DiDi for added safety.

Walking is a great option for exploring Mexico City as it is free, great exercise and a great way to immerse yourself in the city. So, if you're looking for the best way to get around, walking is certainly the way to go.

GETTING TO MEXICO CITY FROM THE AIRPORT

MEX – Mexico City International Airport (aka Benito Juárez International Airport) is the main air gateway to Mexico City. As a major international airport, it has connections to many places all over the world and within Mexico.

Travelling from the airport to the centre of the city takes around thirty minutes and some of the options are;

• **Taxis:** Taxis are the most expensive option, but they offer the convenience of being able to pre-pay at counters in the arrivals hall and avoiding the need to haggle. The cost will be no less than 300 pesos.

• **Uber:** Alternatively, you can use Uber if you have service on your phone. There is a designated ride-share waiting area, and drivers are permitted to pick you up at the airport. Expect to pay around 200 pesos.

- **Airport transfer:** If you would rather book an airport transfer in advance, you can opt for either a private transfer or a shared one, depending on how many people you are travelling with.

- **Metrobus:** Metrobus Line 4 departs from Gates 7 in Terminal 1 and Gate 2 in Terminal 2, and goes directly to Centro Historico. You can buy a smart card ticket at the bus stop for 30 pesos. metro: The airport also has a metro station, however, suitcases are not allowed onboard. Additionally, there are no direct lines to the city centre, making this option slower and less convenient.

As of 2022, NLU – Felipe Ángeles International Airport was opened in Mexico City to provide an alternate option to the existing airport, which had been reaching full capacity for years. This airport is expected to be the destination of more domestic and international flights in the future. It is situated around an hour away from the center of Mexico City, although this could potentially be longer due to traffic. A direct freeway from the city to the airport is currently under construction, and a train will be available starting late 2023. Uber is also in talks about expanding its services to the airport.

Mexico City also happens to be well connected by bus to the rest of the country. Mexico City has four main bus stations located in the north, east, south, and west. Depending on where you are coming from, you can then find the appropriate station. Some of these stations have metro stations connected, making it easy to transfer to the city, while other stations may require a taxi or Uber. Additionally, hundreds of buses leave Mexico City daily, connecting you to plenty of other locations around the country. If you are looking for an easy way to search for the different routes and companies, BusBud is a great option.

For visitors to Mexico City, there is no single best means of transport. It all depends on your budget, the time you have available and your level of comfort in a foreign city. Fortunately, all the options presented in this chapter are safe, cost-effective and easy to use, making it simpler to explore this sprawling yet exciting metropolis and put your mind at ease.

BEST NEIGHBORHOOD TO STAY IN MEXICO CITY- FOR ALL BUDGET TYPES

Navigating Mexico City's vast size and extensive selection of neighborhoods can be an overwhelming task if you're planning a trip to the Mexican capital for the first time. With an area of 1,485 square kilometers (573 square miles) spread across 16 different districts and over 300 neighborhoods, it can be hard to decide where to stay in Mexico City.

When selecting the best area for your trip, you'll need to consider your budget, proximity to public transportation, and, of course, access to the city's top tourist attractions and culinary hotspots. To help make things easier, this chapter will provide a breakdown of Mexico City's most appealing areas and hopefully help you find the perfect fit for your trip.

Overview

Mexico City is one of the largest cities in the world and is home to around 20% of the nation's population. It is situated in the Valley of Mexico (Valle de México) at an elevation of 2,240 meters (7,350 feet), and some visitors may experience some altitude sickness when they arrive, so it is wise to bring some medication along.

The city is built upon the ancient Aztec capital of Tenochtitlan and is a great place to explore the history of Mexico and its modern culture.

Knowing that Mexico City is split into 16 districts (delegaciones), that are then subdivided into over 300 smaller communities (colonias or barrios), will assist you choose where to stay. The districts are a part of several municipalities, or alcaldas.

The most central municipality, Cuauhtémoc, named in honor of a former Aztec leader, is home to several of Mexico City's top lodging options. The city is generally budget-friendly, but there are some 5-star hotels and boutique hotels too. It is important to choose accommodation that is close to the center or a metro station, as traffic in Mexico City can be quite heavy.

Safety is a worry for many travelers when it comes to Mexico City, and while the city is generally safe, there are certain areas that should be avoided. To stay safe and secure, it is best to follow my recommended areas and take extra care when wandering around in the evening.

I've carefully studied and selected the finest neighborhoods to stay in Mexico City based on whether you're on a budget, looking for a luxury stay, wanting to experience local life, or experiencing the city with a young family.

CENTRO HISTÓRICO – WHERE TO STAY IN MEXICO CITY ON A BUDGET

The Centro Histórico area of Mexico City is the perfect destination for tourists who want to explore the city without breaking the bank. Located in the heart of the city, this area offers some of the most iconic landmarks and attractions, such as the Templo Mayor Museum, National Palace, Mexico City Metropolitan Cathedral, and the Palacio de Bellas Artes. Not only is it easily accessible by foot or metro, it also provides a range of affordable accommodation options.

For those looking to experience the city on a budget, the Centro Histórico has plenty to offer. Despite its central location, visitors can find a variety of hotels that are relatively inexpensive for the area. Whether you're looking for a humble hotel or a more luxurious boutique option, you can find something to suit your budget.

Centro Histórico Pros and cons

Pros

- One of the main advantages of staying in the Centro Histórico is the convenience of having all the main attractions within easy walking distance from your hotel.

- Accommodation prices are also quite reasonable considering its central location.

Cons

- On the downside, it can be quite crowded and noisy at night, so be sure to check the exact location of your room before booking.

- Additionally, it is important to be aware of the potential for pickpocketing or other petty theft in this area, especially during the evenings or when visiting Zócalo.

The Best Hotels in Centro Histórico

Mumedi Design Hotel- LUXURY

For those looking for luxury accommodation in Centro Histórico, Mumedi Design Hotel is an ideal choice. Situated close to popular attractions such as the Metropolitan Cathedral of Mexico City, Tenochtitlan Ceremonial Center, and National Palace Mexico, guests can experience the best of the city.

Domingo Santo Hotel Boutique- MID-RANGE

For those looking for something more mid-range, the Domingo Santo Hotel Boutique offers an adults-only experience with a restaurant, bar, and shared lounge. Guests can also explore nearby Palacio de Correos, The Museum of Fine Arts, and Zocalo Square.

Hotel Principal- BUDGET

For those seeking a budget option, Hotel Principal is right in the heart of Mexico City, just a short distance from San Juan de Letrán Metro Station, National Art Museum, Palacio de Bellas Artes Museum, and Constitution Square.

LA CONDESA – WHERE TO STAY FOR FIRST-TIMERS

For first-time visitors to Mexico City, La Condesa is an ideal destination. This lovely area, which can be found in the western part of the city, is made up of the small communities of Condesa, Condesa-Hipodromo, and Hipódromo. La Condesa boasts an array of art nouveau architecture, colorful facades, and tree-lined avenues that all lead to beautiful parks.

Photography lovers can take advantage of the stunning surroundings to capture the perfect shot. Additionally, La Condesa has the benefit of being situated right next to Chatultelpec Park, a large green area containing a boating lake, a European-style castle, botanical garden, and a free zoo. Therefore, this area is ideal for those who want to go for a morning jog or want to bring their family to explore.

Furthermore, La Condesa offers a range of excellent dining options and a lively nightlife scene. When choosing accommodation, there are many options available to suit the needs of each traveler. Not to mention, La Condesa is conveniently situated between Chatultelpec Park and the Centro Histórico, making it the perfect spot for a first-time visit to Mexico City.

La Condesa Pros and cons

Pros

- It boasts a vibrant nightlife scene and a vast variety of eateries
- Accommodation is an attractive prospect making it a great choice for couples seeking something special.

Cons

- Those travelling with children may find it difficult to secure accommodation due to the limited availability of family-friendly options. Thus, it is advisable to book well in advance to ensure a comfortable stay.

The Best Hotels in La Condesa

Casa Malí by Dominion Boutique Hotel- LUXURY

For luxury accommodations in La Condesa, look no further than Casa Malí by Dominion Boutique Hotel. This Mexico City property is situated 1.4 miles from Chapultepec Castle and offers family rooms, a fitness center, a shared lounge, and barbecue facilities.

FlowSuites Condesa- MID-RANGE

For a mid-range stay, FlowSuites Condesa is the perfect choice. Located in the La Condesa district, you can enjoy the area's many restaurants and shops and admire the hotel's elegant, minimalist, and modern decor. Plus, there is a rooftop terrace with a small lounge bar for a refreshing mezcal cocktail.

Casa Decu- BUDGET

For a more budget-friendly option, Casa Decu is conveniently located in the Condesa district of Mexico City. This property is only 1.7 miles from Chapultepec Castle, 1.9 miles from The Angel of Independence, and 2.4 miles from the National Museum of Anthropology. Guests can also enjoy a terrace, a gym, and laundry facilities.

ROMA NORTE- WHERE TO STAY FOR FOOD

Roma is divided into two sections: Roma Norte and Roma Sur. It is a mere hour away by foot to the Zócalo district from Roma Norte, and it is serviced by local metro stations. Foodies will be in their element in this area, as there is an abundance of quality places to explore and enjoy. Roma Norte is renowned for its vivacity and bohemian atmosphere, and is a favourite spot for young Mexicans to live.

Being just a stone's throw away from La Condesa and the Centro Histórico, Roma Norte is an ideal area for those visiting Mexico City for the first time, thanks to its close proximity to these popular attractions and the wonderful selection of eateries.

Roma Norte Pros and cons

Pros

• There are a variety of great food choices and a vibrant nightlife.

• Additionally, it is conveniently located, providing easy access to both the Centro Histórico and attractions further away.

Cons

• The downside is that the hotels in this area tend to be pricier due to its popularity.

The Best Hotels in Roma Norte

Brick Hotel- LUXURY

For those looking for a luxurious stay in Mexico City, the Brick Hotel on Orizaba Street in the La Roma district is the perfect choice. The hotel's stylish restaurant and modern rooms with balconies are just a 5-minute walk from the OMR Gallery and underground access, and 10 minutes from the National Museum of Anthropology. Furthermore, the city's main avenues, Los Insurgentes and Reforma, are within 0.6 miles.

ULIV, Roma Norte- MID-RANGE

ULIV, Roma Norte is a great mid-range option for those wanting to explore the Mexico DF Region. The accommodation is near The

Angel of Independence and the United States Embassy, with Chapultepec Castle 1.2 miles and Museo de Arte Popular 1.4 miles away.

Hotel MX Roma- BUDGET

If you are looking for a budget-friendly option, Hotel MX roma in the Roma district of Mexico City is ideal. It is 1.2 miles from The Angel of Independence, 1.4 miles from the United States Embassy, and 1.7 miles from Chapultepec Castle. Plus, this property offers family rooms and a terrace.

ROMA SUR- WHERE TO STAY FOR LOCAL LIFE

Situated on the opposite side of Coahuila Street, Roma Norte gradually transitions into Roma Sur. Originally, this district was simply referred to as Roma; however, as it started to expand, it was officially divided into two distinct neighborhoods. For those looking to really immerse themselves in the culture of Mexico City, Roma Sur is a great area to explore.

Despite the process of gentrification gradually making its way to this region, Roma Sur still has yet to feel its full effects. Not only is the food scene in this area remarkable, ranging from low-key taquerias to cozy cafes and humble restaurants, but there isn't a huge amount to do or see, making it a great option for expats and digital nomads who are looking for something different on their return to the city.

Roma Sur Pros and cons

Pros

- For those looking for a more local experience in Mexico City, Roma Sur is a great choice
- Plus, if you're planning a prolonged stay in the city or require medical treatment, the area is convenient due to its proximity to various hospitals and clinics.

Cons

- Availability of accommodation is limited and mainly restricted to the southwestern sector of the area.
- Furthermore, there aren't many attractions or activities to enjoy from a touristic perspective.

The Best Hotels in Roma Sur

Fiesta Inn Insurgentes Viaducto- LUXURY

Those seeking the ultimate in luxury should consider a stay at Fiesta Inn Insurgentes Viaducto, located in the heart of the Condesa district, with nearby theaters and nightlife.

Tryp WTC Mexico- MID-RANGE

For those who want to stay closer to the commercial district, Tryp WTC Mexico has much to offer, being only 350 feet from Insurgentes Avenue and a 10-minute walk from the WTC, the Poliforum Siqueiros, and the Pepsi Centre.

Hotel Martí- BUDGET

For those seeking a more economical option, Hotel Martí is situated in the Escandon district, only a short distance from a variety of attractions such as The Angel of Independence, Chapultepec Castle, Chapultepec Forest, the National Museum of Anthropology, the United States Embassy, and Museo de Memoria y Tolerancia.

JUÁREZ/ ZONA ROSA - WHERE TO STAY

FOR LGBTQ+ FRIENDLY ENVIRONS

Juárez is an artistic and vibrant district located to the west of the Centro Histórico. Within Juárez lies the smaller Zona Rosa neighborhood, which has become renowned for its gay-friendly bars, clubs, and karaoke venues. This area is the site of the annual Gay Pride celebration, but also offers a thriving Korean community, making it an ideal place for those who are keen to sample some Korean cuisine or just want a break from Mexican restaurants.

The majority of bars in Juárez are located in the Zona Rosa area, but if you venture away from there towards Chapultepec Park, you will find a number of quiet hotels that are perfect for families. This is also a great place for shopping, with many street vendors selling their artwork, antiques, and other goods. You should also make it a point to wander down Avenida Paseo de la Reforma, which is home to attractions like the Angel of Independence, the Estela de Luz, and Fuente de La Diana Cazadora.

Juárez/ Zona Rosa Pros and cons

Pros

•   Staying in this area can be a great choice, with its abundance of nightlife, shopping, dining and transport options.

•   In Juárez, you can find accommodation at a great price.

Cons

•   When considering where to stay, it is best to avoid booking a hotel in the Zona Rosa area if you are not looking for a lively atmosphere. As it is in the centre of all the activity, the noise may be too disruptive.

The Best Hotels in Juárez/ Zona Rosa

Hotel Geneve CD de Mexico- LUXURY

For those seeking an upscale experience in the heart of Juarez, Hotel Geneve is the perfect choice. This historic building, built in 1907, has been lovingly restored and now offers guests a combination of historic charm and modern amenities. Inside, guests will find free wireless internet, a business center and a state-of-the-art fitness facility, as well as a luxurious spa.

Galeria Plaza Reforma- MID-RANGE

Galeria Plaza Reforma is a distinguished 434 room hotel located in Zona Rosa, just one block from Paseo de la Reforma's office buildings. Guests here can take advantage of the exclusive restaurants, boutiques and shops in the capital city's commercial and financial district.

Posada Viena Hotel- BUDGET

For those looking for a more budget-friendly option, Posada Viena Hotel is a great choice. Located in the center of Mexico City, this hotel offers a characteristic Mexican style and features an Argentinian restaurant on-site. The hotel is just a few minutes away from the Cuauhtémoc Metro Station and Chapultepec Avenue.

POLANCO - WHERE TO STAY FOR A LUXURY VACATION

Polanco is the place to be for those with a penchant for the finer things in life. Here, you will find a wide selection of Mexico City's best Michelin-starred restaurants, like Pujol and Quintonil, as well as luxurious hotels and high-end boutiques. The nightlife is no less elegant, with chic cocktail lounges and wine bars.

Although Polanco is located on the western side of Mexico City, and not as central as some other places, it is nonetheless worth considering if you are spending more than two days in the city, or are returning for a second visit. This is a great area to experience Mexico City from a different perspective. Plus, for honeymooners or those celebrating a special occasion, there is no better place to feel like a king or queen!

Polanco Pros and Cons

Pros

• For those looking to enjoy a luxurious vacation without being too restricted by budget, Polanco is the ideal place to stay in Mexico City.

• It offers a wide array of upscale restaurants, bars and hotels, making it the perfect destination for honeymooners or any couple seeking to indulge in a romantic getaway.

Cons

• The area is somewhat limited when it comes to public transport, with only one metro station in the vicinity.

• Additionally, there aren't many tourist attractions nearby, making Polanco more suited to lifestyle pursuits rather than sightseeing.

The Best Hotels in Polanco

The Wild Oscar- LUXURY

For those seeking a luxurious stay in Mexico City, Wild Oscar provides private residential-style accommodation in the Polanco neighborhood. A restaurant bar, multipurpose rooms, business spaces, private terraces, and a fitness facility are available as amenities. Guests can also take advantage of personalized concierge services, second home services, and business services.

JW Marriott Hotel Mexico City- MID-RANGE

For those seeking a mid-range option, the JW Marriott Hotel Mexico City is five miles from the city center and is a ten-minute walk from the Auditorio Metro Station. The hotel features an outdoor pool, free Wi-Fi, and a Health Club with exclusive spa services. The Xanat restaurant serves Mexican cuisine and the Lobby Bar has a selection of 100 tequilas and a full bar menu.

Rioma Tennyson 86- BUDGET

For those on a budget, Rioma Tennyson 86 is situated in the Polanquito district of Mexico City, and is located near the National Museum of Anthropology, Soumaya Museum, and Chapultepec Forest. The 4-star hotel offers a garden, air-conditioned rooms, free WiFi, and private bathrooms.

DEL CARMEN - WHERE TO STAY FOR FAMILY-FRIENDLY ACCOMMODATION

Del Carmen is a small residential area located in the Coyoacán municipality to the south of the city. Although it has been around for a while, it still preserves a lot of its rustic charm with a variety of lush parks, quaint cafes and bookstores. Art aficionados should not miss the chance to visit the Frida Kahlo Museum, and movie buffs will be delighted by the Cineteca Nacional de México.

One of the top attractions of Coyoacán is Viveros de Coyoacán, a national park filled with trees and pathways cast in the shade of their canopies - perfect for a cool summertime picnic. Further south, the Coyoacán Park (Centro de Coyoacán) boasts many fountains and sculptures of coyotes, paying tribute to the Aztecs who used to inhabit the area long ago. Del Carmen is the ideal location in Mexico City for families who are looking for a peaceful and picturesque place to stay.

Del Carmen Pros and Cons

Pros

• If you are looking for a tranquil and serene respite away from the hustle and bustle of Mexico City's downtown, Del Carmen is the ideal destination.

• Abundant with lush greenery and natural spaces, it is an attractive choice for those travelling with young children.

Cons

• On the other hand, if you are seeking to be at the heart of the action and explore the vibrancy of the Zócalo and nearby neighbourhoods, then Del Carmen is not the most suitable option.

• Accommodation is somewhat limited in the area, it may be worth considering a stay in the Coyoacán district if you are looking for a more central location.

The Best Hotels in Del Carmen

Suites Los Camilos- LUXURY

Experience the highest levels of luxury at Suites Los Camilos, located in Mexico City, just 0.9 miles from Frida Kahlo House Museum. This hotel provides a restaurant, free private parking, a bar, a garden, and a terrace. All of the rooms feature a wardrobe and a private bathroom.

Agata Hotel Boutique & Spa- MID-RANGE

Agata Hotel Boutique & Spa, also in Mexico City, 1,300 feet from Frida Kahlo House Museum, offers mid-range accommodation with a restaurant, free private parking, a bar, and a terrace. Each guest room is equipped with air conditioning, a flat-screen satellite TV, a refrigerator, a kettle, a shower, a hairdryer, and a wardrobe, as well as a private bathroom with complimentary toiletries.

La Casita de Coyoacán- BUDGET

La Casita de Coyoacán offers budget-friendly accommodation with a shared lounge, free private parking, a garden, and a terrace. The hotel also features a 24-hour front desk, a shuttle service, a shared kitchen, and free WiFi throughout.

To finish off, I have provided an overview of the top seven areas to lay your head in Mexico City. My goal is to equip you with the knowledge needed to make a sound judgement when choosing a place to stay. I am confident that you now have a better understanding of the metropolis's various districts and neighborhoods, so you can be more sure of your decision.

THE TOP 27 THINGS TO DO IN MEXICO CITY

A round 10 years ago when I began travelling to Mexico City on a regular basis, some of my friends questioned why. What, they asked, is there to do in Mexico City?

It seems the travel industry is only just beginning to discover the many superb attractions Ciudad de Mexico - or CDMX, as the locals call it - has to offer. It is one of the largest and most vibrant cities on the planet and I have seen many of the world's most famous tourist destinations during my travels.

In truth, there is so much to do in Mexico City that it can be challenging to decide what to do. That's why I am here to help! After my most recent visit to Mexico City, I have put together a guide of the best places to go. I hope you will love Mexico City - by whatever name you choose to call it - as much as I do!

TOP THINGS TO DO IN MEXICO CITY

1.   Palacio de Bellas Artes

Phone: +52 528 647 6500 | Opens from 11am to 5pm, except for Mondays | Entrance is 70 pesos.

Those looking for a stunning architectural experience in the Western Hemisphere should look no further than Mexico City's Palacio de Bellas Artes. This majestic Palace of Fine Arts is located in the heart of the city, adjacent to the lush Alameda Park.

Originally envisioned as a grand National Theater of Mexico to commemorate the 1910 centennial of the Mexican Revolution, the construction of the Palacio Bellas Artes began in 1904. Unfortunately, as is often the case with construction projects in Mexico, it took over three decades to complete.

Today, the Palacio Bellas Artes offers an array of cultural activities and events, such as theatre, opera, dance and art exhibitions. But the best way to appreciate this breathtaking structure is to simply admire it from the outside.

☞ **Pro Tip:** For the ultimate view, travelers should head up to the 8th floor of the local Sears department store. There, they will find a terrace café and spectacular views of the Palacio Bellas Artes perfect for taking memorable photographs. This hidden gem is sure to be a favorite for any Mexico City visitor.

2.   Floating Gardens of Xochimilco

Opens from 8am to 9:30pm daily.

Visiting the Floating Gardens of Xochimilco is a must-do activity when in Mexico City. The gardens are located about 45 minutes away from the city center. This UNESCO World Heritage Site was built upon the ancient Aztec water transport system.

When visiting, you can rent a gondola-style boat and take in the views as you sail down the river. During the two to three-hour cruise, you will be surrounded by other boats, including vendors selling food and drinks.

☞ **How to Get There:** The best way to experience this unique activity is to rent a boat and go with a group of friends. If that is not an option, the next best thing is to go on a tour.

3. Teotihuacan

Entrance fee for adults is 80 pesos and free for children under 13 | Open daily from 9 am to 5 pm.

If you're looking for a unique day trip from Mexico City, Teotihuacan is the perfect destination. This UNESCO World Heritage Site and one of the most visited places in Mexico is home to some of the most impressive ancient ruins in all of Mesoamerica. Built almost 2,000 years ago, these incredible ruins remain remarkably well-preserved to this day.

The main attraction of Teotihuacan is the stunning pyramids, such as the Temple of Quetzalcoatl, the Pyramids of the Moon and the Sun (you can even climb some of them!). Most tours also include a visit to the 16th century Basilica de Guadalupe, which is one of the most famous Catholic religious' sites in the world.

☞ **How to Get There:** If you want to visit Teotihuacan, you can either hire a driver in Mexico City, take a public bus from the Autobuses del Norte station, or join a group tour. For a truly unique experience, you can also book a hot air balloon ride over the ruins.

4.   Chapultepec Park

Opens from 5am until 6pm daily, except Mondays when it is closed

Chapultepec Park is a 686-hectare expanse of greenery located in the heart of Mexico City, with a history stretching back to its use as a royal retreat by the ancient Aztecs. It is a favourite local haunt for families, vendors, and performers, especially on weekends, and is a great place to go walking, running, and biking.

The park is home to the Chapultepec Zoo, the Museum of Anthropology, the Rufino Tamayo Museum, and the Chapultepec Castle, all of which are popular attractions in the city. It is open from 5am until 6pm daily, with the exception of Mondays when it is closed. Unfortunately, this is something I have learnt the hard way, having made the mistake of visiting on a Monday more than once!

5.   National Anthropology Museum

Phone: +52 55 5553 6266 | Opens from 10 am to 5 pm, Tuesday to Saturday | Entrance fee is 80 pesos.

Located at the northernmost point of the Bosques de Chapultepec, the Museo Nacional de Antropología, or National Anthropology Museum, is an extraordinary must-see. Providing extensive ethnographic collections, the museum is an ideal spot to gain insight into Mexico's history. Additionally, the museum's angular modern architecture is an impressive sight in itself, and a great reason to visit.

6.   Plaza del Zócalo

A visit to Mexico City would not be complete without a stop at the Plaza del Zócalo, the city's main square and a place of great historical significance for the country for over 700 years. This plaza is home to important landmarks such as the Supreme Court, the National Palace and the Metropolitan Cathedral, which can all be seen in many iconic photos of Mexico City. Just one block north from the Zócalo lies the ruins of Templo Mayo, another one of the city's must-see attractions.

☞ **An Insider's Tip:** For a beautiful view of the Zócalo, head to the terrace of the Balcón de Zócalo, located at one of the city's finest hotels. Even if you don't stay at the hotel, you can still visit and grab a drink while admiring the view.

7. Museo Nacional De Arte (MUNAL)

Phone: +52 55 8647 5430 | Opens from 10 am to 6 pm every day, closed Mondays.

The Museo Nacional De Arte (MUNAL) is a hidden gem among Mexico City's many cultural attractions. With its grand staircase and lavishly decorated interiors, it's a must-see for anyone visiting the city. Even if the other museums are crowded, this one tends to be relatively quiet.

It's a great place for visitors of all ages to admire the beautiful murals, take a peaceful stroll in the courtyard, and simply take a break from the hustle and bustle of the city. Plus, it's an excellent option for social distancing in mexico city.

8.   Take a Food Tour

☞ Book in Polanco | Or in the Historic Center

If you're looking for the ultimate food experience in Mexico City, you have to try out a food tour. From street food to high end restaurants, you can find several reputable food tours that have been highly rated by past visitors. In particular, the Polanco tour is highly recommended and is a great way to get a taste of different regional delicacies and international flavors in the city. Alternatively, you could also book a food tour in the Historic Center, which is also a great option. Whatever tour you choose, just be sure to come with an empty stomach!

TOURIST ATTRACTIONS IN MEXICO CITY

1. Templo Mayor

Phone: +52 55 4040 5600 | Opens from 9 am till 5 pm, Tuesday – Sunday, Closed Monday

The Templo Mayor, located just a few strides away from the Zócalo in Mexico City, was once believed to be the heart of the universe by the Aztecs. Unfortunately, it was destroyed by the

Spanish to make way for their cathedral, thus marking a dark period in Mexico's history. Despite this, the Templo Mayor was added to the UNESCO World Heritage list in 1987 and has since been remodeled into a museum, consisting of an indoor area and an outdoor excavation site. Sadly, due to an ongoing health emergency, the museum is currently closed, but visitors can still explore the ancient Aztec ruins at the excavation site.

2.   Chapultepec Castle

Phone: +52 55 7601 9811 | Open 9 am to 5 pm daily, closed on Mondays | Entrance is 85 pesos.

Visiting Chapultepec Castle is an absolute must while exploring Mexico City. Situated atop a hill in the middle of the Bosques de

Chapultepec, it is one of only two royal palaces in all of North America; the other being the Palace of Iturbide, also located in Mexico City. Constructed in 1785 upon the instructions of the Spanish Viceroy, the castle has seen a number of alterations over the centuries, including stints as an observatory during the 19th century.

The grounds of the palace are open to the public, with visitors able to take in the spectacular interior and gardens. Wear comfortable shoes if you plan to make the hike up the hill.

3.   Mexico City Metropolitan Cathedral

Phone: +52 55 4165 4052 | Open from 9 am to 5:30 pm every day

The Mexico City Metropolitan Cathedral, created by the Spanish after they demolished the Aztec's central area, is one of the most magnificent Catholic churches in the Western Hemisphere. Spanning 250 years of construction, the outside can be admired from the Zocalo, but the inner complexity is worth a closer look. Inside, the two massive organs will draw your gaze, but remember that photography is not allowed during masses.

4. The Angel of Independence

The Angel of Independence is situated in the middle of a circular road, so it may not be the most thrilling excursion in Mexico City. However, it is certainly a noteworthy attraction and should be included on any itinerary when travelling along the Paseo de la Reforma. Constructed in 1910, it is considered an important symbol and is one of the most well-known landmarks in the city. Photographers should come at night to take some magnificent pictures of the illuminated Angel of Independence.

5.   Soumaya Museum

Phone: +52 55 1103 9800 | Open from 10.30am to 6.30pm each day | Entrance is free

The Soumaya Museum in Mexico City's Polanco district is worth a visit, as it houses a vast collection of artifacts, from ancient objects to modern-day artworks and sculptures. The most popular piece is the 'The Gates of Hell', which is based on the scene from Dante's Inferno. What's more, admission to the museum is free, making it an ideal activity for those on a budget.

Visitors should plan to spend a couple of hours exploring the different floors of the museum. The other two Soumaya Museums located in Mexico City are also worth checking out for those looking for something interesting to do.

6.   Mirador Torre Latinoamerica

Phone: +52 55 5518 7423 | Open from 9 am to 10 pm every day | Entrance is 170 pesos

Visitors to Mexico City have the opportunity to soak up some of the amazing sights the city has to offer, with one of the best spots to take in the views being the observation deck of the Torre Latinoamerica skyscraper, located near the Palacio de Bellas Artes. Admission to this magnificent spot is 170 pesos, which allows access to some interesting museum exhibits, but the real draw here is the stunning views of Mexico City. If you're trying to save money, there is a café situated two floors below the observation deck that also offers incredible views at no cost.

7.   Frida Kahlo Museum

Phone: +52 55 5554 5999 | Open daily from 10am - 6pm, except for Mondays | Entrance fee for foreign tourists is 270 pesos.

If you're looking for a unique cultural experience, why not visit the Frida Kahlo Museum, known as 'Casa Azul' for its blue exterior. This museum, located in her former house, offers an insight into her personal life, her relationship with Diego Rivera and her battle with the crippling effects of polio. You'll find a few of her pieces of artwork, as well as artifacts from her home, including her specially made dresses which had to be designed to accommodate her frail figure.

☞ **Pro Tip:** It's important to note that the museum is a popular attraction in Mexico City, so you should purchase your timed-entry tickets several days in advance.

8.   Trotsky Museum

Phone: +52 55 5658 8732 | Admission is 40 pesos | Open from 10 am to 5 pm daily, closed on Mondays.

The Trotsky Museum in Mexico City is a great attraction for fans of history. The house, located in the Coyoacan neighbourhood, was once the home of Leon Trotsky, the famous Marxist revolutionary and political theorist, who was murdered in the Mexican capital in 1940. Although it is closed at the time of writing due to the health crisis, prior to this it was a popular tourist destination.

Unlike the Frida Kahlo museum, the Trotsky Museum is less crowded and offers visitors a chance to get an insight into the life of the influential communist leader.

FUN AND UNIQUE THINGS TO DO

1.   Palacio Postal

Phone: +52 55 5512 0091 | Open from 8am to 7:30pm on weekdays, 10am to 4pm on Saturdays and 10am to 2pm on Sundays

The Palacio Postal in Mexico City is a great spot to take photos, especially when there are fewer people around! The building is still a working post office, so while you're there you can post any packages and then take a moment to appreciate the intricate artwork that decorates the building. It's a fantastic free activity when you're in Mexico City and definitely worth checking out.

2.   Lucha Libre

If wrestling is your thing, or you simply love a good show, then you'll love going to a lucha libre match. The luchadores really put on a show, and the audience is always wildly enthusiastic.

Arena Mexico is one of the larger venues for these matches, and you can buy tickets yourself online, or take part in a tour specifically designed for foreigners who want to experience the thrill of a lucha libre match, but with someone to guide them through the throng of fans.

3. Licorería Limantour

Phone: +52 55 5264 4122

If you are looking for some of the best cocktails in Mexico City, then Licorería Limantour is the place to go. Located in Roma Norte, the bartenders here are among the most talented in the country and the atmosphere is always lively, no matter which night of the week you visit. There is also a smaller outpost in Polanco, although it is recommended to make a reservation in advance.

FREE AND LOW-COST ACTIVITIES TO DO

1.   Churrería El Moro

Multiple Locations | Four churros start at 93 pesos

Travelling to Mexico City should include a visit to Churrería El Moro, a well-known chain that has multiple outposts in the city. Indulge in the delicious churro, a fried doughy snack coated in sugar and drenched in different chocolate sauces. No trip to Mexico is complete without a sample of this scrumptious dessert.

2.   CDMX Signs

Taking a photo of the "CDMX" signs is an obligatory activity for visitors to Mexico City. These signs, which signify Ciudad de Mexico, can be seen in various areas, especially in the Zocalo. Capturing a picture of the sign ensures that your journey to the Mexican capital is documented. So be sure to take out your camera when you spot one of these "CDMX" signs!

3.   Casa de los Azulejos

Phone: +52 55 5512 1331 | Open between 7am and 1am every day

The Casa de los Azulejos, commonly referred to as the House of Tiles, is an eighteenth century Baroque palace located in the downtown historic district of Mexico City. It is home to numerous restaurants and shops, as well as a picturesque interior courtyard.

The building is particularly impressive for its exterior which is decorated with stunning Instagram-worthy blue and white tiles. Situated close to the Palacio de Bellas Artes and Avenida 5 de Mayo, it is the perfect place to visit for those exploring the attractions of the city.

4.   Mercado de Artesanías La Ciudadela

Phone: +52 55 5510 1828 | Open from 10am to 7pm on weekdays (closes at 6pm on Sundays).

If you are looking for an authentic and unique Mexican souvenir, the Mercado de Artesanías La Ciudadela, situated in the vicinity of the historic center, is the perfect place to explore.

At the market, you will find vendors from all over Mexico, selling their artwork and various products to both locals and tourists. Many of the vendors accept credit cards, but if you pay in cash, you may be able to get a bargain.

5.   Plaza Garibaldi

Open 24 hours

Plaza Garibaldi is the ultimate destination in Mexico City for a memorable experience. This lively spot is open 24 hours a day, giving people the freedom to explore the vibrant energy of the city at any time. During the day, visitors can take a break from sightseeing and enjoy a delicious lunch while listening to some mariachi music. As the day turns to night, the plaza becomes the perfect place to grab a few drinks and take in the mariachi sounds.

6.   Avenida 5 de Mayo

Avenida 5 de Mayo is a pedestrian street that plays an integral role in the city. It is surrounded by many of Mexico City's points of interest, as well as a wide array of shops. From large retailers like H&M to local vendors, this street provides visitors with plenty of shopping options.

7.   UNAM Central Library

Phone: +52 55 5622 1625 | Open from 8:30am to 9:30pm daily

The Central Library at the National Autonomous University of Mexico ("UNAM") is a great place to visit in the Coyoacán neighborhood of Mexico City. It is particularly popular for the beautiful, vibrant and detailed murals adorning the exterior. Each mural portrays a different period of Mexico's history, ranging from pre-Hispanic to the modern era and the history of the university. The architecture of the library is also interesting and worth exploring. Best of all, it's a great budget-friendly activity for visitors to the city.

8.   Museo Soumaya- Casa Guillermo Tovar de Teresa

Phone: +52 55 1103 9800 | Open from 10:30am to 6:30pm every day | Entry is free.

Nestled between Condesa and Roma, the lesser known Museo Soumaya- Casa Guillermo Tovar de Teresa is a small yet stunning house museum. Its proprietor, Guillermo Tovar de Teresa, lived an extravagant life and exploring the elaborate interior and admiring the artwork, furnishings, and design is an effortless way to spend your time in Mexico City without spending a dime.

That concludes this chapter; you now have an idea of what to do in Mexico City!

NIGHTLIFE IN MEXICO CITY

The vibrant nightlife of Mexico City offers something to suit all tastes, from supper clubs with floorshows to ritzy piano bars, rusticantros, and bars playing traditional Mexican music. La Condesa and La Roma are the places to be to experience the best of what the city has to offer, but Juárez has recently become a bohemian hotspot. Zona Rosa and Polanco are also well-known nightlife destinations.

It's important to be aware that the altitude can have a significant impact on the body's reaction to alcohol, and you may find yourself feeling more intoxicated than usual. Additionally, there is a risk of crime in the capital after dark, and it is advisable to guard your belongings carefully in crowded nightlife areas.

Mexico City has a long cultural history with many art forms, including pre-Hispanic folk art, the works of the 20th-century muralists, and the music and literature of hip-hop poets, graffiti maestros and classic Mexican romantics. One of the most popular musical genres is mariachi, where groups of musicians' serenade passers-by with their tunes.

BARS IN MEXICO CITY

Baltra Bar

If you're looking for a hip, bohemian atmosphere while in Mexico City, Baltra Bar is the perfect place to go. A talented mixologist works at this quaint and friendly establishment, creating unique beverages like the Twinings tea-based cocktail collection.

Address: La Condesa, Iztaccíhuatl 36D, Mexico City,

Telephone: +52 55 5264 1279.

Website: http://baltra.bar

La Coyoacana

If you want to experience a more traditional cantina, La Coyoacana in Coyoacán is the perfect spot to visit. This nostalgic spot features delicious food, great mezcal and an inviting atmosphere. Featuring rustic furnishings and décor, you can also find live music.

Address: Higuera 14, Coyoacán

Telephone: +52 55 5658 5337.

Website: http://lacoyoacana.com

The Beer Box

The Beer Box is a business that is already highly respected for its selection of Mexican beers. But they don't just stop there; they also have a great selection of American craft beers, as well as brews from other parts of the world. The Beer Box in Juárez has a modern and chic atmosphere to match its impressive selection of drinks.

Address: Juárez, Londres 216, Mexico City,

Telephone: +52 55 5207 7441.

Website: http://www.thebeerbox.com

CLUBS IN MEXICO CITY

AM Local

AM Local is a well-known nightlife spot in the Condesa district of Mexico City. It is especially popular among fans of House, Techno and Electronica music. This place often has guest DJs from around the world, so a night out here will be one to remember.

Address: Avenida Nuevo León 67, La Condesa

Telephone: +52 55 2079 1283.

Website: http://localam.com

Mama Rumba

Mama Rumba is a great place to experience salsa in Mexico City, especially for those who are just starting to learn the passionate and lively dance. On Wednesdays, free classes are available at 8pm, followed by a club session that starts soon after.

Address: Roma Norte, Queretaro 230, Mexico City,

Telephone: +52 55 5564 6920.

Mono

Mono is a fantastic spot for electronic music at an affordable price. It can get crowded, so if you don't want to stand in line, try to visit midweek.

Address: Juárez, Versalles 64, Mexico City,

Telephone: +52 55 2666 8474.

Website: http://www.mono.am

LIVE MUSIC IN MEXICO CITY

Bar El Jorongo

For the past 25 years, Bar El Jorongo has been acclaimed as one of the best nightspots in the city. Referred to as the 'House of Mariachi', this music venue draws some of the most renowned Mexican musicians to its atmosphere.

Address: Cuauhtémoc, Sheraton Maria Isabel Hotel, Paseo de la Reforma 325, Mexico City,

Telephone: +52 55 5242 5555

El Imperial

El Imperial is still considered one of the trendiest music spots around. Its prices are competitive, drinks are top-notch, and its antiquated ambiance creates an unlikely setting for a rock club. Yet, it remains a popular destination for its customers.

Address: Roma Norte, Avenida Álvaro Obregón 293, Mexico City,

Telephone: +52 55 5525 1115.

Website: http://elimperial.tv

Salón Tenampa

If you're seeking a truly authentic Mexican musical experience, head to Plaza Garibaldi in the Centro Histórico district. Located between Republica de Honduras and Republica de Peru, you'll find this tree-lined square filled with mariachi bands playing until the early morning hours. If you come between 8pm to midnight, you'll be able to witness groups of musicians in their iconic black and silver-studded suits and wide-brimmed hats. Salón Tenampa is a renowned establishment in the plaza - customers can enjoy drinks and be serenaded by mariachi musicians.

Address: Centro Histórico, Plaza Garibaldi 12, Mexico City,

Telephone: +52 55 5526 6176.

Website: http://www.salontenampa.com

ESSENTIAL SPANISH PHRASES TO KNOW BEFORE TRAVELING TO MEXICO

If you don't have any knowledge of Spanish prior to travelling to Mexico, it would be a wise decision to learn a few words and phrases before you go. In most of the well-known vacation spots, it is likely that you will find people working in the tourist industry who speak English, but if you go to more isolated areas, having some Spanish will be of great help. Get yourself a good phrasebook (or even an app) and make sure to use it regularly. You will most likely come across lots of people who will try to understand what you need, even if they don't speak English. Nevertheless, no matter where you visit or whether the people you meet understand English, making the effort to speak a little Spanish can bring you closer to the Mexicans you encounter.

Meeting New People

1.   **¡Hola!** - Hello!

2.   **¿Cómo estás?** - How are you?

3. **Mi nombre es Mira** - My name is Mira

4. **¿De dónde eres?** - Where are you from?

5. **¿Cuál es tu pasatiempo favorito?** - What is your favorite hobby?

6. **¿Cuál es tu profesión?** - What is your profession?

7. **Es un placer conocerte.** - It's nice to meet you.

Going Out for Food or Drinks

1. **¿Qué hay para comer?** - What's there to eat?

2. **¿Qué hay para beber?** - What's there to drink?

3. **¿Dónde está el mejor lugar para comer?** - Where can I get the best food?

4. **¿Puede sugerirme algo?** - Can you suggest something?

5. **¿Cuál es el plato típico?** - What is the traditional dish?

6. **¿Cuáles son los precios?** - What are the prices?

7. **¿Puedo ver la carta?** - Can I see the menu?

Asking for Directions

1. **¿Dónde está...?** - Where is...?

2. **¿Cómo llego a...?** - How do I get to...?

3. **¿Cuál es el camino más corto?** - What is the quickest route?

4. **¿Puede mostrarme en el mapa?** - Please locate for me on a map

5. **¿Está cerca de aquí?** - Is it close by?

6. **¿A qué distancia estamos?** - How far away are we?

7. **¿Puede darme indicaciones?** - Can you give me directions?

Getting Medical Attention

1. **¿Estoy enfermo?** - Am I sick?

2. **¿Qué tengo?** - What do I have?

3. **¿Cuáles son los síntomas?** - What are the symptoms?

4. **¿Necesito una receta?** - Do I need a prescription?

5. **¿Cuánto me costará?** - How much will it cost?

6. **¿Dónde puedo conseguir medicamentos?** - Where can I get medicines?

7. **¿Puedo ver a un médico?** - Can I see a doctor?

Basic Mexican slang

1. **¡Órale! – Ooh-rah-lay!** This phrase is used to express excitement or show support.

2. **¡Qué chido! – Kay-chee-doh!** This is basically the same as saying "cool!"

3. **¡Epa! – Eh-pah!** This is said to show admiration or surprise.

4. **¡No manches! – No-man-chays!** This is used to express disbelief or frustration.

5. **¡Aguas! – Ah-gwahs!** This phrase is used to warn someone to be careful or watch out.

6. **¡A huevo! – Ah-way-vo!** This phrase is used to express agreement or agreement with enthusiasm.

7. **¡Ay, caramba! – Ay-car-ahm-bah!** This is used to express surprise or dismay.

THE PERFECT MEXICO CITY ITINERARY FOR 7 DAYS

Navigating a city as big as Mexico City can be overwhelming but with the right approach and planning, you can make the most of your trip. This 7-day itinerary has all the must-see sights and experiences you need to have an unforgettable holiday.

You'll start your journey exploring all the best neighbourhoods to explore and sights to see, as well as savouring the tastiest food. You'll also have time for must-do day trips, and have enough relaxed time to wander around and experience the city like a local.

It's important to note that many of the museums and ruins around the city are closed on Mondays. This includes popular attractions such as Templo Mayor, the Frida Kahlo museum and the Anthropology Museum. That being said, there are still plenty of activities and places to visit that remain open such as Roma Norte, Condesa, Teotihuacan and Polanco. The Soumaya Museum also doesn't close on Mondays.

With 7 days, you can enjoy the best of Mexico City and discover the hidden gems. Whether you're looking for an adventure-filled holiday, a cultural experience or simply a relaxing break, this itinerary has something for everyone.

DAY 1 – GO BACK IN TIME TO CENTRO HISTORICO

The majority of historical landmarks are found in Centro Historico, which is perched on the remains of the ancient Aztec city of Tenochtitlán. Spend a day of sightseeing in this culturally significant neighbourhood and observe the throng of tourists and locals alike, who come to bask in the grandeur of the past.

Day 1 – Morning

Begin your exploration of Mexico City's Centro Historico, the beating heart of the city, with a visit to one of two well-known restaurants. El Cardenal offers a traditional Mexican breakfast served in a grand and historic setting, while the cheaper option of Pasteleria Ideal has been a popular icon for almost 100 years and is filled with delectable pastries and baked goods.

After breakfast, Head to the Zocalo, or Plaza de la Constitucion, for a glimpse into the city's past. As the largest central square in the world, it has been a gathering place for centuries and, today, continues to host political and social protests. You can't miss the Mexican flag flying high above the square.

Adjoining the plaza is the Catedral Metropolitana, the largest cathedral in Latin America. Built in a range of different architectural styles, it is possible to go inside and admire the ornate ceiling and stained glass windows.

Also adjacent to the Zocalo is the iconic Palacio Nacional, home to the famous mural 'The History of Mexico' by Diego Rivera. Be sure to take a peek inside before making your way to the Templo Mayor, the ancient Aztec temple situated across the plaza. Do bear in mind that there is a strict policy about bringing food or drinks into the ruins and museum, so you should finish off any snacks from Pasteleria Ideal before entering. It is also advisable not to purchase any water prior to entering, as it will likely be confiscated by the gatekeepers.

Palacio Nacional

The Templo Mayor is the remains of the impressive structure that once stood at the heart of the city of Tenochtitlán, which Mexico City was built on top of. You can explore the ruins and the on-site museum, which is surprisingly large and interesting; allow yourself at least an hour here, even if you're not a history enthusiast. Although not necessary, it can be advantageous to join a tour with a local guide to gain a greater appreciation of the temple, as you'll be able to understand the stories behind the ruins with their explanations. The tour usually includes skip-the-line entry and around 90 minutes of exploration.

Day 1 – Afternoon

Now that your appetite is likely awakening, make your way to lunchtime with some stops along the way. Exit the Zocalo and head down the pedestrian-only Avenida Madero. You'll find a plethora of shops, markets and street vendors, which are teeming with tourists. Be sure to take a photo in front of the Casa de Los Azulejos (House of Tiles) and its ornamental tiles.

If you're looking for a hearty Mexican lunch on a budget, Taqueria Los Cocuyos is the place to go. Recommended by Netflix's Taco Chronicles and also by the culinary king Anthony Bourdain, these tacos are incredibly delicious! This inconspicuous hole-in-the-wall taqueria can be easily identified by the long lines queuing in front of it. Expect to find succulent, fatty and delicious tacos.

Alternatively, if you'd prefer to dine in a more formal setting, you can't go wrong with Sanborns. The location of this restaurant is worth the visit, as it is housed in the picturesque House of Tiles.

Once you've replenished, take a stroll over to the Palacio Postal (Postal Palace) and be amazed by the stunning Art Nouveau interior. Make sure to look up to the stained glass ceiling as you ascend the marble staircase. There is a separate entrance for those simply looking, so you can avoid the lines of locals using the postal services.

Afterwards, make your way to one of the most iconic sights of Mexico City, the Palacio de Bella Artes (Palace of Fine Arts). This majestic marble building is dedicated to the fine arts, and inside you'll find a concert hall and arts centre. You can enter the building for a small fee, but it's best to see it from the outside. Visit Finca Don Porfirio on the eighth floor of the nearby Sears building to have a drink while enjoying the view of the Palacio.

Take some time to explore the verdant Alameda Central, one of Mexico City's oldest parks. During springtime, the park is awash with a beautiful purple hue as the Jacarandas bloom. To behold the beautiful view of this sprawling metropolis, ascend to the 44th floor of the Torre Latinoamericana (Latin America Tower) and explore the viewing deck. You can also leave and re-enter on the same day and witness the city lights at night. If you're not keen on the viewing deck, then you can make your way to Miralto, the bar on the 41st floor, and buy yourself a drink with your pesos.

Alameda Central

For a quick visit, make sure to drop by Mexico City's Barrio Chino (Chinatown). Even if it's not the world's biggest Chinatown, the streets of Calle Dolores are lined with colourful lanterns and umbrellas, and you can pick up some scrumptious steamed buns if you're feeling a little peckish.

Barrio Chino (Chinatown)

Day 1 – Evening

After a long and exhausting day of exploring Centro Historico, the perfect way to unwind and take in the sights is to visit the Balcon del Zocalo, a rooftop bar with an unbeatable view of the plaza and cathedral. Enjoy a refreshing drink as you watch the sun set for the evening.

Taqueria Arandas is a great option for a quick and casual dinner before heading home. For those who are still feeling energetic, Plaza Garibaldi is a must-see. This is the home of many Mariachi bands and the atmosphere is electrifying. Witness the well-dressed musicians performing traditional Mexican songs and dance along with the crowd. However, it is important to note that the neighbourhood near the plaza is quite impoverished, so in order to see everything and stay safe, it is preferable to go on a guided tour with a local expert.

DAY 2 – VISIT THE HIPSTER HANGOUTS OF ROMA NORTE AND CONDESA.

The neighbourhoods of Roma Norte and Condesa, known for their leafy streets and vibrant atmosphere, are a world away from the frenetic activity of the Centro Historico. In the past, these areas were popular with hipsters and those who followed a bohemian lifestyle, and they are now considered to be the most fashionable places in Mexico City. But despite their popularity, they have kept their chilled, alternative vibe. It is almost impossible to believe that you are in a capital city of 22 million people, such is the serenity of the surroundings: beautiful cafes, lush trees and bright, multi-coloured homes, with the birds singing in the background. These areas are side by side, so you can easily take in both of them in one day.

Day 2 – Morning

Begin your day in the vibrant neighbourhood of Roma Norte. Exploring on foot or by bicycle is the best way to experience this area - and you can rent a two-wheeler from the city's shared bike Ecobici. It's not hard to see why this is such a popular part of town for cyclists, with its wide boulevards and dedicated bike lanes.

Even though there are a few locations worth visiting, the best way to enjoy Roma Norte is to wander and savour the atmosphere.

Before you get started, make sure you have a filling breakfast. This neighbourhood is full of unique cafes, and brunch is the go-to option. Lalo! is a great spot, with its cheerful murals and fabulous breakfast menu - we recommend the French toast. If you'd prefer something to take away, Panadería Rosetta is the place to go - it's a beloved local business, renowned for its delicious bread and pastries.

Take a walk down Avenida Alvaro Obregon after eating breakfast. This is the main street, lined with coffee shops, boutiques and a picturesque tree-lined sidewalk. Look out for the street art, and admire the beautiful colonial houses. Although the main attractions of the city are located in neighbouring Condesa, there are still some places worth seeing in Roma Norte - such as Plaza Luis Cabrera, Plaza Río de Janeiro and the Fuente de Cibeles (Fountain of Cybele).

Plaza Río de Janeiro

Day 2 – Afternoon

It's time to make your way to the neighbouring Condesa. Start your journey at Parque España, a picturesque green space that is home to hundreds of dogs during the weekdays. Pet owners hire trainers and dog sitters to look after their four-legged family while they are at work. The park is equipped with off-leash enclosures so the dogs can play, run and interact with each other. It is fascinating to watch the dogs obediently follow the instructions of their trainers and remain still in their line. Every once in a while, some of the dogs get impatient and try to break the formation, but their trainers soon bring them back in line with just a look. If you are a dog person, then this park is a must visit.

Parque España

Before you leave the park, don't forget to check out the Parque España Audiorama. This is a community area managed by the city and is a peaceful spot for people to come and relax. You can find books to read, comfy chairs and lounges, and calming music. It is a great place to rest your feet and take a break.

For lunch, Koku is a great spot. This Japanese restaurant has a beautiful courtyard with delicious rice bowls. If you are in the mood for tacos, then El Tizoncito is the place to go. They are said to be the inventors of the renowned al pastor tacos.

After lunch, visit Parque Mexico. Similar to Parque España, you will witness more dogs, a quiet audiorama, and tree-lined paths. Then wander back to Roma Norte and stop at a Cafebreria El Pendulo for a quick refreshment. This chain of bookstore-cafes offers a great opportunity to take a break from sightseeing.

Day 2 – Evening

Tonight, Mercado Roma is the place to be for dinner. This modern take on a food market offers a variety of international and Mexican food stalls, as well as bars serving up tasty cocktails. Explore the stalls to pick something you like, or go upstairs to the rooftop bar to enjoy a drink.

If you're looking for more entertainment, Roma Norte and Condesa are the perfect places to party, offering some of the city's best bars and clubs. Make sure to check out Mama Rumba for a night of salsa dancing. This Cuban salsa bar provides dance classes for beginners on Wednesdays and Thursdays at 8 pm, before the music starts and the crowds start rolling in.

No Mexico City trip is complete without late-night tacos, and Taqueria Orinoco is open all night long! They serve three types of classic meat tacos – trompo (pastor), res (arracherra) or chicharron – at an affordable price and in no time.

DAY 3 – CYCLING ACROSS THE CITY AND CRUISING THE XOCHIMILCO CANALS

We would strongly recommend arranging this day to take place on a Sunday, if it is feasible. Modify your plans if necessary to ensure this day falls on a Sunday - there are several reasons to do so. On this day, you will be biking along the Paseo de la Reforma, Mexico City's main avenue that is shut off to all cars on Sunday mornings. Afterwards, you will be able to take a tour of the nearby Juarez district, before enjoying a cruise on the renowned Canals of Xochimilco in a vivid gondola-style boat.

Day 3 – Morning

On Sundays, Mexico City's Paseo de la Reforma, one of the busiest roads in the city, is closed off to cars. This is part of the city's Muevete en Bici initiative to get people to get out and about, exercising and spending time with family and friends. While you can rent bikes from stalls that are set up specifically for the day, you can also use the EcoBici bike-sharing system.

Paseo de la Reforma

This landmark avenue is Mexico's version of the Champs-Élysées in Paris and links Centro Historico to Chapultepec Park. It consists of a wide road, lined with leafy pedestrian areas on either side, as well as bike lanes. Along the avenue, visitors can also find some of the tallest buildings in the city and a number of monuments and statues, such as the gold Angel De La Independencia and the Fuente de la Diana Cazadora.

Fuente de la Diana Cazadora

Even if you don't join the Muevete en Bici, it is still worth visiting Paseo de la Reforma, as well as the Juarez neighbourhood. After your exploration, you can also follow the locals' lead and go for brunch in Juarez. Jardín Chapultepec has a weekend brunch in their garden, while Farmacia Internacional is a favourite spot for coffee, bread and pastries.

Day 3 – Afternoon

Visiting the Floating Gardens of Xochimilco in Mexico City should be at the top of your list when exploring the city. The canals are the last remaining evidence of the complex system of waterways built by the Aztecs for the ancient city of Tenochtitlán.

Cruising the canals in a brightly painted trajinera boat is a fun activity for both locals and tourists alike, and there are plenty of tour options available if you'd like the ease of having everything organised. However, it's perfectly possible to explore the area independently. The easiest way to get there is to take the metro to Tasqueña station and then switch to the Tren Ligera light rail that runs to Xochimilco station.

Once you arrive, make your way to the embarcaderos (piers), where you'll find plenty of trajineras and captains waiting to take you out on the canals. It's worth noting that the cost is capped by the government at 500 pesos per hour, so be sure to haggle if the captain offers a higher price. Two to three hours is plenty of time for a trip, and don't forget to bring snacks, drinks and a speaker if you have one.

The atmosphere on the canals is particularly lively on Sundays, when boats are full of families celebrating various occasions and vendors row up alongside to offer refreshments. And if you're lucky, you might even encounter a mariachi band ready to board and serenade you with a song.

Day 3 – Evening

After you return to the city, make sure to take some time to explore the Juarez neighbourhood at night. A stroll down the Paseo de la

Reforma is a completely different experience when lit up after dusk, and you'll find some fantastic eateries in the area.

Paseo de la Reforma at Night

Juarez is especially renowned for its selection of Korean and Japanese restaurants; Wan Wan Sakaba is a great choice for some delicious, authentic Japanese food, from ramen and rice bowls to sushi. Alternatively, if you're craving tacos, the Taqueria La Palmera is a cheap, traditional Mexican restaurant with an inviting al pastor trompo smoking out front. Lastly, if you're up for it, the Zona Rosa (pink zone) in the Juarez neighbourhood offers a vibrant nightlife scene.

DAY 4 – EXPLORE THE LUXURY POLANCO

Polanco, the affluent district of Mexico City, is the place to be for those wanting to be in the spotlight. It is home to an array of renowned eateries, exclusive designer stores, and lavish shopping centers, setting it apart from the more rustic Centro Historico.

Day 4 – Morning

After three hectic days in Mexico City, take it easy this morning. Have a leisurely breakfast in or near your accommodation and then use either Uber or the Metro to get to Polanco station. Polanco is one of the wealthiest areas of the city, and a great place to spend some time people-watching or imagining yourself in one of the grand houses.

Start your exploration at Parque Lincoln, a long, leafy park, then move on to Avenida Masaryk, the area's main road, filled with posh stores, fancy restaurants and swanky cars. The streets are all named after famous authors, so take the time to wander down them and admire the flower-filled alfresco areas and leafy, European-style streets.

Also, be sure to check out the Insta-famous 'Mexico Mi Amor' neon sign in front of the TANE jewellery store.

Mexico Mi Amor Neon Sign

Day 4 – Afternoon

Today's lunch in Polanco promises a delightful taste of Mexican cuisine, and Taqueria El Turix is the perfect place to start. Famous for its Cochinita Pibil, a slow-cooked pork traditionally from the Yucatan area, the taqueria is a hole-in-the-wall taco place with a reputation for quality. Add a panucho, a fried tortilla stuffed with refried beans, and the experience is complete.

After your delicious meal, continue your adventure with a trip to the iconic Museo Soumaya. This six-floor museum is owned by Carlos Slim Helú, one of the wealthiest people in the world, and admission is free! Explore artworks from around the world and admire the unique architecture from the outside.

To crown your day in Polanco, a visit to Churreria El Moro is a must. This beloved chain has been serving up mouth-watering churros and hot chocolates for almost a century, and with two branches in the area, you can enjoy the best of the best.

Day 4 – Evening

Polanco is home to some of the finest restaurants in the world, and it's definitely worth treating yourself to a meal even if you're on a budget! The Michelin restaurant guide doesn't cover Mexico, but if it did, Mexico City would certainly have at least two restaurants included in their list! Other worldwide restaurant rankings consistently feature some of the most exquisite restaurants in the city.

Pujol is one of the most popular restaurants in the city, currently sitting at #5 in the 'World's 50 Best Restaurant' list. It serves a seasonal tasting menu, whilst their renowned mole is a permanent feature.

Restaurante Pujol

Located close by is Quintonil, which is run by a former chef from Pujol. Similar to the other restaurants on the same list, it offers a tasting menu that emphasizes traditional Mexican foods with a contemporary twist. It is ranked at #9.

Mexico City Travel Guide 2023

Bookings for both of these restaurants are highly recommended, so it's best to make your reservation weeks or even months in advance.

DAY 5 – GET AWAY FROM THE CONCRETE JUNGLE AT CHAPULTEPEC

Bosque de Chapultepec, often regarded as Mexico's version of Central Park, is an enormous 4 square-kilometer park that serves as the lungs of the city. It is not just an ordinary park; it contains a range of attractions that are renowned around the world, such as museums, landmarks and beautiful sights. A day trip to this park should be a top priority for any traveler's 7 day Mexico City itinerary.

Day 5 – Morning

Start your day by making your way to the Bosque de Chapultepec (Chapultepec Forest). The main entrance is not far from the Chapultepec Metro Station, or you can take an EcoBici bike and cycle up Paseo de la Reforma to enter the park. There are many trails and gardens to explore, so take your time and enjoy the scenery.

To get the full experience, make your way up the hill to Castillo Chapultepec (Chapultepec Castle). This 18th century castle was the home of Mexican royalty, including the Emperor Maximilian I. Now a museum, visitors can explore the grounds and learn about the castle's rich history. Don't forget to take in the incredible views of the city skyline from the checkered tile balcony.

To finish your visit, rent a swan-shaped paddleboat and take a leisurely ride around Lago de Chapultepec (Chapultepec Lake).

Chapultepec Lake

Day 5 – Afternoon

The lake is conveniently located beside the Zona de Comida, a great spot to get lunch with several restaurants and food stalls. Afterwards, head over to the Museo Nacional de Antropología, an amazing museum to learn more about Mexico's ancient civilisations such as the Aztecs and Mayas.

You'll need the majority of your afternoon to explore the museum, seeing all the interesting artefacts and interactive exhibits. Read all the signs, although some of them may be in Spanish. If you don't speak Spanish, you can use your phone and Google Translate to take pictures of the signs and convert them to English. Remember the museum is closed on Mondays!

Day 5 – Evening

Tonight is the night for a true Mexican cultural experience - Lucha Libre! It's much more than just Mexican wrestling - it's full of colour, costumes, acrobatics and passionate fans, so it's sure to be a night of fun and laughter.

Wrestling matches are held at two arenas - Arena Mexico and Arena Coliseo - and usually start later in the evening. You can check the schedules online on the arena websites, or you can get tickets in advance online, on the night from the ticket office, or you can even organise a guided tour which will take care of the tickets and offer transport to and from the stadium.

DAY 6 – STROLL AROUND VIBRANT COYOACAN.

Coyoacan is an oasis of tranquility, situated only a short distance away from the bustling city centre. Here, the streets are lined with a kaleidoscope of colonial-style buildings, sporting a Bohemian atmosphere, accompanied by a sedate tempo. The streets are adorned with lush greenery, and the cobblestone roads add to the idyllic charm.

Day 6 – Morning

This morning, why not take an Uber or hop on the metro (Coyoacan station) to the neighbourhood of Coyoacan? Start your day right with a cup of coffee or hot chocolate at Terra Garat; they use Mexican coffee beans and cacao. The Casa Azul (Blue House), the former residence of Mexican artist and feminist Frida Kahlo and her husband Diego Rivera, which has since been transformed into the Frida Kahlo Museum, is well-known across the world. Here you can see many of Kahlo's belongings, as well as some of her artworks. In order to visit Casa Azul, be sure to book your tickets online in advance and select the day and time you would like to visit, as it is closed on Mondays.

Apart from the museum, there are plenty of other vibrant and colourful houses to explore in the area. Make your way to the heart of Coyoacan, where you can discover Plaza Hidalgo and Jardin Centenario.

Day 6 – Afternoon

When you've got the munchies, head over to Mercado Coyoacan. It's home to the renowned Tostadas de Coyoacan, who boast that their tostadas are the best in the area! With that taken care of, spend the rest of your day however you please. Maybe take a stroll around your favourite neighbourhood, have a picnic in one of the city's parks or just take some time out in your accommodation.

Day 6 – Evening

This evening is the perfect opportunity to explore the delectable flavors of Mexico City! From tacos and tortas to tamales and beyond, the food here is some of the best in the nation. This tour is your chance to explore the local cuisine with a local, who will take you through markets, backstreets and small street food stalls to uncover some of the city's most delicious dishes. Not only will you sample a variety of popular tacos all around the city, but you'll also be able to taste some traditional mezcal and Mexican craft beer.

After all the food, you'll be ready to hit the sack, especially since you have an early start tomorrow.

DAY 7 – SOAR ABOVE THE ANCIENT CITY OF TEOTIHUACAN

Visiting Teotihuacan, the ancient Mesoamerican city located nearby the centre of Mexico City, is a must for anyone exploring the area. The city is home to some of the largest pyramids in the world and a hot air balloon ride above it is an incredibly unique experience to add to any itinerary.

Day 7 – Morning

On the final day of your 7-day Mexico City tour, you will be up early, but it will all be worth it when you witness the sunrise while soaring over the 2,000-year-old pyramids in a hot air balloon. Sky Balloons MX is one of the reputable companies that offer this experience, and they provide transportation from the city, so you'll be collected around 4:30am.

Teotihucan from a hot air ballon

Once you reach the port, you will be able to observe the colourful balloons filling up and taking to the sky. When your balloon and captain are ready, you will climb into the basket and take off. For the next 45 to 60 minutes, you will be able to fly over the ancient

143

city and marvel at the Pirámide del Sol (Pyramid of the Sun) and Pirámide de la Luna (Pyramid of the Moon) from above. It is an incredible sight to behold and will be an unforgettable memory for you.

When the captain skillfully navigates the hot air balloon back to the ground, you will be able to celebrate with a champagne toast. Most companies also provide a buffet breakfast at a nearby restaurant after the flight.

Day 7 – Afternoon

Ensure that your travel arrangements are organised so that you have enough time to explore the incredible city of Teotihuacán on foot. Despite being widely mistaken for an Aztec city; Teotihuacán was actually built by an ancient Mexican civilisation that remains a mystery to us. The city is quite small but its main street, the Calzada de los Muertos, is over 2 kilometres long and connects the Pyramid of the Moon to the Quetzalcoatl Temple. Allow yourself two to three hours to wander around and admire the remarkable structures that have stood the test of time.

Regardless of whether you take a hot air balloon ride or not, this site is definitely worth a visit. Before heading back to Mexico City, have lunch at La Gruta, a unique restaurant set inside a cave that serves traditional pre-Hispanic cuisine. The atmosphere is also quite special, with the cave lit up by candles.

Day 7 – Evening

On the concluding night of your stay in Mexico City, the possibilities are endless! Reacquaint yourself with a cherished eatery, go on a nocturnal jaunt throughout some of the most renowned locales, or explore a number of the city's top-notch bars. Whatever your preferred pastime, the night is yours to enjoy!

Finishing off our 7-day Mexico City getaway, we were so glad we had come! There's so much to do and see in the giant urban area, we were sure a week would be enough to get a good glimpse into the city's culture and attractions. Even though you could easily choose to stay for longer and still not experience everything the city has to offer, we hope that this week-long visit gave you a good understanding of what makes Mexico City so amazing.

Hope you enjoyed your read.

Please kindly leave a review.

....

YOU MAY ALSO ENJOY OTHER BOOKS FROM THE AUTHOR:

PRAGUE TRAVEL GUIDE 2023: 70+ Ultimate Prague Experiences (With Pictures), Your Guide to All You Need to Know, where to Go, what to Do and Local Tips.

DUBAI, UAE TRAVEL GUIDE: 70+ Ultimate Dubai Experiences (With Pictures), Your Guide to All You Need to Know, where to Go, what to Do and Local Tips. (Middle Eastern Travel Guide)

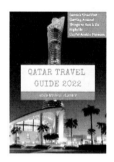

QATAR TRAVEL GUIDE 2022: 40+ Ultimate Qatar Experiences (With Pictures), Your Guide to All You Need to Know, where to Go, what to See, what to Do and Local Tips.

Made in United States
North Haven, CT
10 July 2023

38774310R00083